A CENTURY
OF STORIES
NEW HANOVER COUNTY PUBLIC LIBRARY
1906-2006

CRICKETS

by Liza Jacobs

New Hanover County Public Library
201 Chestnut Street
Wilmington, NC 28401

San Diego • Detroit • New York • San Francisco • Cleveland • New Haven, Conn. • Waterville, Maine • London • Munich

For more information, contact
The Gale Group, Inc.
27500 Drake Rd.
Farmington Hills, MI 48331-3535
Or you can visit our Internet site at http://www.gale.com

Photographs © 1997 by Lee Chin-Hsing

Cover Photograph © CORBIS

© 1997 by Chin-Chin Publications Ltd.

No. 274-1, Sec.1 Ho-Ping E. Rd., Taipei, Taiwan, R.O.C.
Tel: 886-2-2363-3486 Fax: 886-2-2363-6081

LIBRARY OF CONGRESS CATALOGING-IN-PUBLICATION DATA

Jacobs, Liza.
  Crickets / by Liza Jacobs.
    v. cm. — (Wild wild world)
  Includes bibliographical references
  Contents: About crickets — Chirping — Mating — Pets.
  ISBN 1-4103-0045-5 (hardback : alk. paper)
  1. Crickets—Juvenile literature. [1. Crickets.] I. Title. II. Series.

  QL508.G8J23 2003
  595.7'26—dc21
                                                              2003001465

Table of Contents

About Crickets 4

Chirping 6

Sensing and Reacting 8

Mating 10

Egg-Laying 12

Three Stages of Growth 14

Molting 16

Above and Below Ground 18

Many Kinds of Crickets 20

Caring for Crickets 22

For More Information 24

Glossary 24

About Crickets

Crickets live in many parts of the world. Like all insects, crickets have three main body parts—the head, thorax (midsection), and abdomen (rear section).

They have long antennae and six legs. Although many crickets have two pairs of wings, they cannot fly. Instead, male crickets use their wings to communicate. They do this by rubbing the underside of one wing against the upper side of the other wing. Only males can chirp. Females have smooth wings and cannot chirp.

① ② ③ ④

Chirping

Male crickets chirp for three reasons—
to attract a female, while fighting with
another male, and to claim something
belonging to them (territory or food).
Crickets eat a lot of different things,
including insects, seeds, vegetables,
fruit, and even pieces of cloth. They
use their strong jaws to crunch up
their food.

7

Sensing and Reacting

Many kinds of animals eat crickets, including lizards, birds, snakes, frogs, raccoons, mice, and insects such as beetles and praying mantises. Crickets have two sensors, called cerci, at the end of their abdomen. They also have tympanums, or "ears," that look like white dots. There is one on each of their front legs.

Adult crickets hide when they hear or sense an animal coming near. They can also use their strong back legs to jump up to 2 feet away to escape attack! Little spines on their legs help crickets get a good grip when climbing through grasses and leaves.

Mating

Male crickets rub their wings together to attract females for mating. The chirping sound made is sweeter than the one a male makes when fighting. The male and female study each other's face and antennae before mating. To mate, a male crawls underneath a female. They may stay this way for several hours.

Female crickets have a
long, egg-laying tube with
a sharp tip that comes out
from the end of their
abdomen. This is called
an ovipositor. When a
female finds a place to lay
her eggs, she digs holes in
the ground with the tip of
her ovipositor.

①

②

12

Egg Laying

A female digs several hundred holes. She passes a single egg into each hole as she goes. Cricket eggs are yellow and tube-like. The holes are covered with dirt to protect the eggs from the cold, and from animals that would otherwise eat them.

Three Stages of Growth

Crickets go through three stages of
life as they grow into their adult forms.
The first stage is the egg. Then a baby, or
nymph, hatches from the egg. Its color
is pale, but it will darken as it
ages. Unlike adult crickets,
nymphs do not have fully
formed wings.

① ②

It takes a month
or more for a
nymph to grow
into an adult.

Larvae ① ②

Molting

Insects have a hard covering over their bodies called an exoskeleton. The more nymphs eat, the more they grow. Like other insects, a cricket s exoskeleton does not get bigger as the insect grows. In order to grow to its adult size, a cricket has to shed its covering several times. This is called molting. The old skin splits open and the cricket wriggles out with a new, larger covering! Its exoskeleton is soft at first, but quickly hardens.

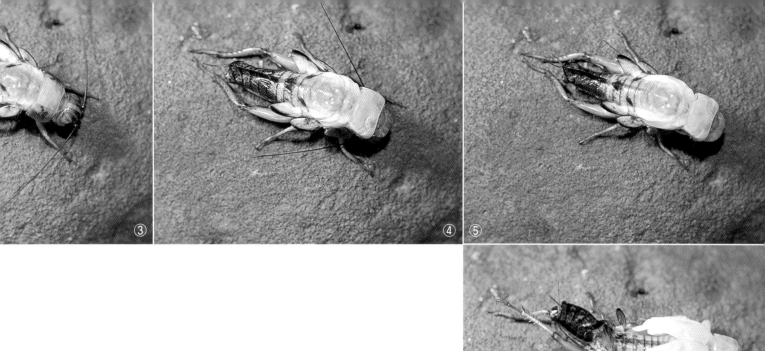

③ ④ ⑤

⑥

⑦

Nymphs often eat their old shell. After its last molt, a cricket is a fully grown adult.

⑩

⑨

⑧

Above and Below Ground

Crickets can be found in several different parts of one area. They like places that are damp. In a forest or garden, crickets might live in a burrow they dig under the ground, or be found living in a bush, under a rock, or in a rotted log.

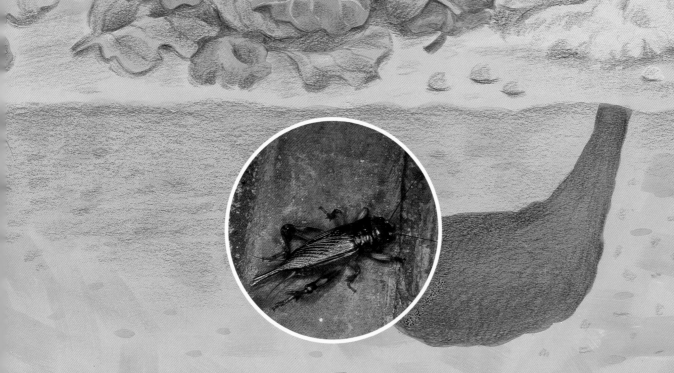

Many Kinds of Crickets

There are hundreds of different kinds of crickets. They are found in different sizes and colors. Most are brown or black. Others are pale green. Some crickets have colorful markings.

Caring for Crickets

Some people like to keep crickets as pets. A home can be set up for crickets using a small fish tank, some dirt, and several places for the crickets to hide. Make sure the lid lets in air and fits tightly—crickets can jump high! Crickets can be fed food scraps, fruits, vegetables, seeds, and certain kinds of pet food, such as rabbit pellets. They will also need water. Crickets are easy to take care of as long as you give them the food and shelter they need. And their chirping makes them very musical guests!

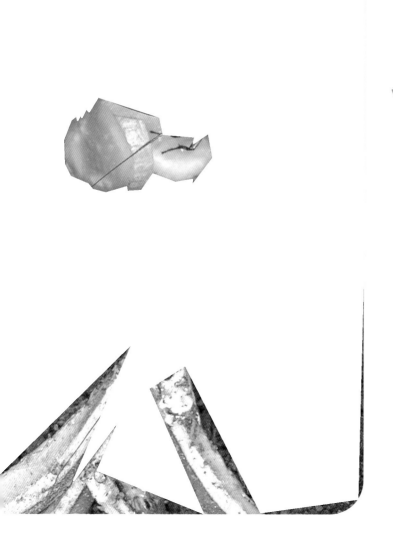

For More Information

Berger, Melvin. *Chirping Crickets (Let's-Read-and-Find-Out Science).* New York: HarperTrophy, 1998.

Miller, Sara Swan. *Grasshoppers and Crickets of North America.* Danbury, CT: Franklin Watts, 2002.

Pascoe, Elaine. *Crickets and Grasshoppers (Nature-Close-Up).* San Diego, CA: Blackbirch Press, 1998.

Glossary

cerci two sense organs that come from the end of a cricket's abdomen

exoskeleton the hard covering on the outside of an insect's body

molt to shed the outer skin or covering

nymph the second stage in a cricket's life

ovipositor the reproductive organ through which a cricket lays her eggs

tympanum ear membrane found on the front legs of a cricket